THE DURHAMS IN KOREA

The 1st Battalion The Durham Light Infantry in the Korean War 1952-53

Harry Moses

Published by
COUNTY DURHAM BOOKS

ACKNOWLEDGEMENTS

In writing this history of the 1ˢᵗ Battalion DLI in Korea, I am indebted to many people who listened to and answered my many questions or who provided written reminiscences & photographs of their service in Korea. Amongst these were Brigadier Peter Jeffreys DSO, OBE [who also allowed me to use his private papers]; Brigadier Robert MacGregor-Oakford CBE, MC; Colonel Eric Burini; Colonel Hugh Sawbridge OBE; Colonel John Lightley; Colonel Michael Mcbain, Colonel David Dunn, Major R.S Clarke MBE, MC; J Coley, Fen Davison, Ernest Dobson, Bryan Dolman, William Hedges, J Jobson, Ted Jones, Alfred Mason, Alan Mavin, J Murray BEM, John Scott, Ernest Stockton and Robert Stockton MM.

This history would never have been written without the support of Steve Shannon, manager of the DLI Museum & Durham Art Gallery, who made available to me the documents, maps, photographs & Regimental Journals covering the activities of 1 DLI in Korea and who also edited the final narrative.

The DLI's archive, including the Korean papers, is now held at the Durham County Record Office and I would like to thank the CRO's staff for their cheerful help in locating and copying photographs.

Finally, I would like to thank Margaret Brooks and Peter Hart of the Imperial War Museum for permission to quote from taped interviews with Eric Burini, Ernest Dobson, John Lightley, Alan Mavin & John Scott.

ISBN 1897585 72 1

FOREWORD

Brigadier **Peter J. Jeffreys** DSO & BAR, OBE

This excellent booklet records the activities of the 1st Battalion in one of the earliest of the post war conflicts; a period in the history of The Durham Light Infantry which earned them the respect, admiration and comradeship of our cousins from Australia, Canada, India and America. Our reputation as a fighting unit was of the highest order and was entirely due to the fighting qualities of the men of the Battalion. That these same men were almost 85% National Servicemen among the junior ranks of both men and officers speaks volumes about the recruiting areas from which they came. Though, initially, I was concerned about the possible outcome of our tour in Korea before our arrival, in the event my concerns were groundless, the National Servicemen proved to be resilient and cheerful in the most trying circumstances, and did not let me down once.

The Light Infantry system of brigading proved to be of immense value and was well organised in that we were able to call upon ample reserves who made their way through the system to be available whenever required. The quality of these reinforcements was of equal worth whichever Light Infantry Regiment provided them. I was, and still am, extremely proud to have been given command of the 1st Battalion during this crucial period in the history of The Durham Light Infantry; I am happy to recommend this booklet to all those who belong to the Regiment, especially the many veterans who can regard the year they spent in far off Korea with pride and a sense of achievement which they richly deserve; they are the men who made the Battalion what it was and The Durham Light Infantry what it still is.

I must congratulate Harry Moses on producing this booket and hope that everyone who remembers those days will want to read it, refer to it often and recall the comradeship that they experienced.

INTRODUCTION

The Korean War began on 25th July 1950. Over the next two years the conflict ebbed and flowed - first in favour of the North Koreans who advanced to the far western corner of South Korea before they were finally held in front of Pusan. Then the landing of the United States X Corps at Inchon and attacks out of the Pusan bridgehead turned the tables on the North Koreans and the United Nations forces advanced north almost to the Chinese frontier. The Chinese then intervened in October 1950 and, with their North Korean allies, drove the UN forces back south. Later fighting saw the front line finally established about the line of the 38th Parallel. Although severe fighting continued, a near stalemate was reached by early summer 1951 and the two fronts became stabilised and well dug in. Most fighting was then limited to local objectives and became very like trench warfare of WW1. Peace talks opened in July 1951, transferring to Panmunjon on 25th October. This was the situation when the 1st Battalion The Durham Light Infantry arrived in Korea on 7th September 1952.

IF I'D KNOWN YOU WERE COMING I'D HAVE BAKED A CAKE

The 1st Battalion DLI left Berlin on 30th May 1952, arriving at Brancepeth Camp early in June. Three weeks leave was then granted. On 3rd June, Lieutenant Colonel Peter Jeffreys DSO, OBE took command. A local newspaper journalist wrote: *The Commanding Officer of the Battalion, Lieut Colonel Jeffreys, was serving in Germany as a Colonel when offered the post and, although it meant dropping in rank, he immediately accepted – "as anyone would," to quote his words. He is extremely popular with his men in whom he has the greatest faith. The general view of the men themselves about going to the battlefield is that it is "just something that has to be done." Perhaps it was all put in a nutshell by RSM Fred [Batter] Edwards, who said briefly, "Someone has to finish it."*

Private Coley, Machine Gun Section, summed up the men's opinion of their new CO. *Colonel Jeffreys was great. He was a good officer. We saw him every day. If he didn't come and visit you personally, he would pass and wave. He knew where every man was. He knew every man by name. He knew your exact positions. He knew your targets. He was absolutely marvellous and very well liked.*

On 30th June, after leave had ended, the battalion moved to Bellerby for training on the surrounding moors. This included erecting barbed wire, setting and firing explosives, digging-in, firing weapons on the range, route marches and company schemes. On 12th July, the Durhams were taken in trucks to West Auckland. From there, they marched 15 miles through Bishop Auckland, Spennymoor and back to Brancepeth Camp. The Regimental Band met them and played them through each town with the residents cheering them on their way. It had become well known that they were about to go to Korea.

On Sunday 20th July, a service was held in Durham Cathedral, followed by a march through the city streets. One local journalist wrote:

Cheering and hand clapping greeted the 1st Durham Light Infantry - who are leaving on July 29th for service in Korea - as they paraded through the city on Sunday for a farewell service at the Cathedral. It was a warm farewell that they were offered, for people standing five deep in the narrow streets, jostled each other to catch a glimpse of the lads who soon no doubt will be living up to, and increasing the reputation of one of the country's finest regiments. They provided an inspiring sight as they marched from Elvet at their traditional cracking pace, and they will leave their country safe in the knowledge that they fill a large part in the hearts of so many people, for it is many years since such a crowd was seen in Durham on a Sunday.

After the service, the troops formed up on Palace Green and marched down to the Market Place, where the Lord Lieutenant of the County, Lord Lawson of Beamish, took the salute.

It was soon time to leave for Southampton but not before some of the Durhams arranged a fitting departure. Private Fen Davison wrote:

Around 27ᵗʰ July, Company Orders read "The Company will parade at 1830hrs. Dress Battle Order. CSM Hawksworth inspected and roll call carried out. We were then informed: Muster Parade again at 1930hrs and roll call again taken by Platoon Sergeants. We were then fell out and told to muster again at 2100hrs, the same routine except we were to be ready to move in the early hours of the morning.

Leaving Southampton on the 'Empire Trooper', July 1952.

7

Being the first company to fall out, we decided to run down as quickly as possible to the 'Shafto Arms' in Page Bank, down past the assault course, over the football pitch. I looked back and saw the rest of the company behind. It was like a cross-country run. Rushing into the quiet bar, I asked for four pints and said, "You had better start filling - the whole battalion is behind me." I think he thought I was kidding until he saw all the khaki figures bursting through the door.

We mustered in the early hours of the morning and then marched to Brancepeth Station, where the troop train awaited us. Finally, all the battalion was aboard, we moved off looking out of the windows, taking a last look at Brancepeth. I think some of the chaps had never been in a train before and, watching them walk back and forwards along the corridor, they must have walked all the way to Southampton.

At Southampton, the Regimental Band was waiting on the quayside. Second Lieutenant Hugh Sawbridge was involved with loading and reloading kitbags, he wrote:

We had to offload two kitbags for soldiers who cannot now travel. Typically, they are the last two to get off the vans. We're surrounded by the Dock Foreman and his gang,

Disembarking at Pusan, 7th September 1952.

who wonder why we are doing their work..."Much quicker," we muttered...the Foreman was much impressed by our speed – light infantry pace! We parted the best of friends.

The battalion boarded the 'Empire Trooper' - a converted German liner captured in 1939 - and set sail, as the Band played and crowds cheered. The Durhams packed the ship's rails acknowledging the waves and cheers. The boat was also packed with drafts, not only for Korea, but also for Port Said, Aden, Ceylon, Singapore and Hong Kong. At sea, the troops were kept busy with daily deck inspections, boat drill, physical training, weapon training and furnishing fatigue parties. On 14th August, they went ashore at Aden for a 6-mile route march, in conditions described as *"hot as hell"*. Shore leave was given at Colombo, Singapore and Hong Kong. At Hong Kong, reached on 2nd September, the officers were entertained by the Colonel of the Regiment, Lieutenant General Airey.

The Durhams finally landed at Pusan, Korea on 7th September 1952, where the ship was welcomed by a US Army Band – all tall, black soldiers in gleaming white helmets - who played "If We'd Known You Were Coming We'd Have Baked A Cake" - much to the amusement of everyone.

REGULARS & NATIONAL SERVICEMEN

In Korea, the 1ˢᵗ Battalion DLI became part of the 28ᵗʰ Commonwealth Brigade, 1ˢᵗ Commonwealth Division. Initially, it was brigaded with the 1ˢᵗ Battalion Royal Fusiliers and the 1ˢᵗ & 3ʳᵈ Battalions Royal Australian Regiment, supported by 16th Field Regiment RNZA, 61st Light Regiment RA, 60th Indian Field Ambulance and Norwegian MASH.

Second Lieutenant Sawbridge later listed the **Order of Battle** of 1 DLI in Korea –

CO:	Lieutenant Colonel P.J. Jeffreys DSO, OBE
2i/c:	Major C.R.W. Norman OBE
Adjutant:	Captain R.E.G. Scott – later transferred to 'D' Coy
Asst. Adjutant:	2/Lieutenant H.E. Dynes
Padre:	Reverend R.H. Pattinson RAChD
RSM:	WOI F.G. 'Batter' Edwards

HQ Company:

OC:	Captain E.C. Ellis
QM:	Major G. Flannigan MBE, MM
MTO:	Captain A.T. Taylor
WTO:	Captain M.L.N. Benson MC
SO:	Captain J.B. Tonkinson – later Adjutant. 1953/54
IO:	Lieutenant P.S. Hayes – later Captain W.J. Nott-Bower
MO:	Captain L.J.H. Arthur RAMC
CSM:	WO2 Lambert – later W.O.2 Scott
RQMS:	WOI Reece
AQMS:	WO2 Cole

'A' Company:

OC:	Major C.P. Donoghue MC – killed in action 2.1.1953
	Major R.S. Loveridge MC from 3.1.1953

'B' Company:

OC:	Major R.G. Atkinson MC

'C' Company:

OC: Major G.B. Whitworth – till December 1952
Major J.A. Tresawna DSO – from December 1952
Major G.B. Griffiths - 11th June 1953 on death of Major Tresawna

'D' Company:

OC: Major J.W. [Sean] Kelly – wounded 2nd October 1952
Major R.E.G. Scott

'S' Company:

OC: Major R.S. Loveridge MC – till 3.1.1953
Major A.J. Taylor from 3.1.1953
Captain E.B. Burini [3" Mortar Platoon.] – later Captain D.A.G. Arnott
Lieutenant P.M.de W. Greenwell [MMG Platoon.] – later Captain J.G. Burkmar
Lieutenant C.F. Bower [A/Tk Platoon.]
Captain N. Hodgson [Assault Platoon.]
CSM WO2 L. Beirne

[from left] Major Atkinson, Lieutenant Colonel Jeffreys, General Airey, Brigadier Daly, November 1952.

This Order of Battle changed regularly as officers came and went. Amongst those who joined the Durhams later was a young officer - Second Lieutenant Peter de la Billiere. As there were a number of 'Peters' in the battalion, he was re-christened 'Eddie' and, as the soldiers could not get their tongues around his surname, he became known as 'Eddie Smith'. Later Lieutenant General Sir Peter de la Billiere KCB, CBE, DSO, MC became one of the nation's most gifted and famous army commanders and commanded the British contingent in 'Operation Desert Storm' - the war against Iraq. Initially, the make-up of the battalion gave Lieutenant Colonel Jeffreys some concern. Nearly 50% were National Servicemen. His fears were quickly dispelled. After the war, he wrote:

The National Service Subaltern. What an excellent job he did! He seemed to mature about a year for every two months he was in Korea. And those who had been with the Battalion eight or nine months were a sad loss when they left. By that time, they were most of them masters at the exacting task of managing men in their daily trench life, organising their work and leading them on patrol... 10 of them were wounded and 1 killed.

The National Service Other Rank was as great a success, if not greater, than the Officer. Before going into action I was apprehensive that the qualities of toughness and self assurance would be lacking in the very young men we had brought. Of their enthusiasm, discipline and general military efficiency, I was certain, but could they compare with the confident mature Australians with whom we were brigaded, and with the brave resourceful expert field craftsmen that their enemy had proved himself to be? I need have had no qualms on this, or any other count...the Battalion quickly settled to war and the youthful National Serviceman changed in a few short weeks to a mature, self-reliant, imperturbable fighting man...The tough cheerfulness and spiritual strength these men showed speaks volumes for the country's future...Many National Servicemen made good NCOs. They provided about 40% of the Battalion's full corporals, and six became excellent Sergeants.

National Servicemen served for a fixed period and then left for home on the termination of their engagement. They were then replaced by others recently arrived in Hong Kong, where training was provided by the Royal Ulster Rifles. When old enough these young National Servicemen were moved to Japan where they trained at the Divisional Battle School before finally being sent to Korea. The Durhams were rarely up to full strength largely due to these changes.

Lance Corporal Alan Mavin was one of these replacements:

A lot of the lads who'd done the first half, they were coming home for demob. You've got to remember that you had six weeks to get out there on the boat. You had six weeks to come back, there's twelve weeks of your time taken up travelling. If you'd already done six months or nine months before they took you out there and you'd done another six months there, the National Service was ending. That's why we were going out, not for the dead or the wounded. We were going as replacements for the National Servicemen. They were coming home. But you had to leave three months before you were due for demob.

These young officers and other ranks depended upon the experience of the regular officers. Lieutenant Colonel Jeffreys wrote:

The Regular soldier is naturally the backbone of the Battalion. He provides the comparative permanence to a shifting population; in our case a little over one-third of the total Other Rank

RSM 'Batter' Edwards, 1 DLI.

strength. His influence is substantial and he carries a considerable responsibility for a battalion's standard of performance. As regards Officers, the quality in Korea was more than adequate. Warrant Officers, Colour-Sergeants and Senior Sergeants also did excellently. No praise can be too high for them. The 1st Battalion DLI was fortunate to have company commanders and officers of other senior rank who were Regular soldiers and highly experienced through action in World War II.

BRITANNIA CAMP

O n disembarking, the battalion boarded the Korean Communications Zone Train [K-Comms Comet], for the journey to Britannia Camp. Second Lieutenant John Lightley, commanding No.4 Platoon 'B' Company, remembered:

We got onto this appalling railway, the worst train you could possibly imagine, no lights, no windows, hard seats, no toilets - just a hole in the floor. We travelled for an hour then stopped for two hours, travelled for an hour, stopped for two hours. It was dreadful. You had to have a guard on each door to the carriage, with Bren guns, because there were supposed to be North Korean infiltrators who might attack the train.

The journey took two days and it was a pretty browned off battalion that reached Britannia Camp on 9th September. This tented camp was for acclimatisation and training before going into the line. Set in a chestnut wood, there were only basic amenities. However the weather was good and the Durhams settled in quickly. During this time, training intensified, weapons were inspected and all attended Royal Engineer lectures on mines, minefield construction, field defences and bunker construction. Officers from the Royal Australian Regiment, already experienced in the line, gave talks on the enemy tactics and patrolling.

The land around the camp featured steep scrub-covered hills with rice fields in the valleys and the Durhams

Captain Burini & Major Donoghue MC, 1952.

practised patrolling up hills and down. Tactical training in both attack and defence also took place, whilst night exercises involved the location and recognition of terrain. Slit trenches were dug with overhead cover and wiring and revetting practised. To keep fit, there were route marches. Weapons were fired. Captain Eric Burini, commanding the Mortar Platoon on arrival in Korea, met with early problems:

I began as Mortar Officer, an appointment I had held in Germany, where the weapon was reasonably accurate. However my first experience on the same weapon in Korea almost destroyed my belief in its use. I found that, having ranged with great difficulty some targets, when I called for mortar fire the bombs fell over an area of some 300 square yards and not one on the targets previously ranged. I never did find out why this was so. Nevertheless this dispersal of bombs did prove useful later when the CO asked me to put down a smoke screen behind the two forward companies. The smoke screen satisfied the CO, thank God, and proved to be my last operational effort as Mortar Officer. When we left the line, I handed over to John Arnot and took over as 2ic to Pat Donoghue, OC 'A' Company.

TRENCH BEAUTIFICATION - LIFE ON POINT 159

On 24th September, 1 DLI moved into the line near Naechon and onto Point 159. Private William Hedges, Assault Pioneers Platoon, had an early experience of the Australian soldier:

Within a few days of our arrival in Korea, some of us went into the front line in advance of the Battalion to join the Australians and learn the position of the minefields in front of what was to become our position. Before going in that night, we were given a lecture telling us that, after reaching the road-head by trucks, we would be met by an Australian guide who would take us to the trenches. From then on there would be no talking, no noise, no smoking and no lights.

It was quite a surprise, therefore, when we reached the reverse slope of 'our hill' to

Point 159, Korea.

find the Australians sitting round a bonfire, singing, smoking and drinking beer. I was allocated a 'hoochie' [dugout in the hillside] with three Aussies. The roof was so low we had to stoop. When I suggested that we dig the floor out to give us more headroom, they said, "You will have as much headroom as you want by the end of the week." Little did I know that the floor was boxes of Japanese beer and, as the days went by, the floor got lower. They were great blokes to be with. The Best.

The main battalion followed the advance party. The weather was appalling. Private Ernest Dobson of 'A' Company remembered:

For the ride up we got into these American wagons, it was bucketing down. I think this was where it really hit us. I think we were all frightened because it was raining, the heavens opened up. Everyone was trying to get to the back of the wagon for a run-off. It was fright. I think this is what sticks in my memory. It rained right up to the dropping off point. We got off and formed up. We were going into the front line, taking over from the front company Royal Australian Regiment and we had to march there, full gear and everything. It was black dark. You had to try and keep in touch with the bloke in front. You were slipping down. Honest! What a night! They reckoned it was a good night to take over, as there wouldn't be much activity going on in front of you. By the time we got up to the front line, I was fed up. I bet it took over an hour to get from the Reserve Company, up to where we had

Lance Corporal Scott, 1 DLI.

17

to go, easy, maybe longer with the conditions. We began to realise this was the real thing.

Lance Corporal John Scott remembered the reception they got from the Australians and the Chinese:

We went into this dugout, a section out, a section in. All the Aussies were saying, "You poor Pommie bastards". That's how we were greeted moving in. We heard the sound, "Welcome 1ˢᵗ Battalion DLI" from the Chinks. We thought "Eh! How did they know this?"

Captain R.S. Clarke remembered the arrival of his company in the line:

'D' Company was positioned on one of the forward hills facing the Chinese on a similar line of hills across the valley. On this particular day, shortly after our arrival in the line, enemy artillery and mortar fire was directed on us and early on Sean Kelly was wounded and had to be evacuated. As second-in-command, I took over and as the day wore on, shelling intensified. In the evening, I had warned the platoon commanders that all this shelling might be the prelude to one of their attacks on our position and if the shelling suddenly intensified, as it would in such an event, they were to get their men out of their 'hoochies' and man the trenches so as not to be caught like rats in a trap when the Chinese overran our position.

Soon after they had returned to their platoons, it started and one of our companies on a hill behind us had the spectacle of 'D' Company disappearing in a cloud of dust and smoke. Of course, the noise of exploding shells on our position can be imagined. I thought this was it and was glad that I had, at least, told the platoon commanders to man the trenches! After about half an hour of intense bombardment, it suddenly stopped as suddenly as it had started. There was a dead calm. What could all this mean? On investigation, I discovered that we had suffered hardly a casualty and I have it on record that the Chinese on the hill opposite, were standing up and roaring with laughter. All they had done was to take the mickey out of a green battalion they knew had just moved into the line! It was obvious that the North Korean intelligence system was well served by its many agents throughout the countryside.

Life on Point 159 set the pattern for the rest of the campaign – a company placed on a hill and ringed with barbed wire and mines. From this position, the valley could be covered by patrols and by mortars and Bren guns operating on fixed lines. The battalion's arrival unfortunately coincided with the end of a relatively quiet period. Then men could move around, even stand on the parapet without attracting fire from the enemy opposite, but the increased enemy activity necessitated an improvement in the Durham's positions.

Lieutenant Colonel Jeffreys wrote:

Our first task was to dig hard - field works in fact remained one of our main preoccupations during the whole of our tour. They provided the one certain and effective answer to enemy harassing fire. No training in the completion of defensive positions has been undertaken in the British Army for many years; no experience had been available since 1918, but when the necessity drives, people soon learn. One laughable aspect of the matter is that everything we learnt had been learnt by our fathers in 1914-18. Suffice to say that from the day we went into the line until the day the cease-fire sounded we never ceased to dig hard. The simple essence of the business was to have a six to eight foot trench system from which radiated fire trenches or weapon pits. On the reverse slope of the hills were the dugouts, ideally with five feet of head cover and constructed of stout, shaped timber that the Divisional Engineers provided in pre-fabricated sets.

So, like their forebears in WW1, the battalion dug. Second Lieutenant Lightley remembered:

The first priority was to make sure the section weapon pits were in good order. We used a standard design based on the length of the steel pickets used for wiring. At each end of the pit were shelter bays to provide cover and to store ammunition. The roofs were supported by pickets and had a good cover of rock and earth. All the walls were revetted with sandbags and pickets. Sandbags were laid as

In the trenches, Korea.

carefully as bricks and the Company Commander, Reggie Atkinson, made regular visits to inspect the quality of the work: shelves for grenades, protected from rain by hessian, wooden pegs on the parapet to aid night firing and drains to keep everything as dry as possible.

Previous occupants had not been too particular about camouflage and hygiene, so our first jobs were usually to clean up the litter, such as tin cans, which surrounded each trench. Latrines were essential in a static position. Reggie insisted that they had to be self-consuming, which in practice meant that they had to be about 6ft. deep. This was quite a problem in frozen ground. No one lingered on the 'loo' as they were always out in the open and prone to the odd mortar bomb. It also meant undoing your warm clothing and risking frostbite!

The importance of good and clean trenches had much to do with the efficiency of the battalion and Lieutenant Colonel Jeffreys set the highest standards as he outlined:

Picture a man living in a trench often in cold, wet or hot weather: he has a pit or a fire trench from which to fight; he lives with four others in a dark dug-out; his clothes and himself are difficult to keep clean; so are his weapons; the disposal of rubbish; of urine; etceteras, present great difficulties...feeding is not easy; and he lives in these conditions day in day out for at least three weeks at a time. Unless a very high standard of discipline is combined with a willingness and a determination to triumph over conditions, the standard of living will be too low to sustain health, morale, equipment, efficiency or administrative organisation...Trenches must be spotless [we used even to brush the floors of all trenches with home-made brooms]. All ammunition must be neatly stacked in caches in the trench side; shaving, washing, cleaning boots, brushing equipment, must all come as second nature, difficult though this may be [it was never too cold to strip to the waist and wash, and how everyone laughed over it on a really freezing morning!]. Urinals must be sunk into the trench side, latrines require particular care to make them sanitary, comfortable and safe. And above all, cooking must be first class; the Platoon cookhouse in a dug-out was much the best answer though not many battalions adopted it.

The Australians coined a phrase for this - 'trench beautification.'

The larger shelters dug into the sides of the hill on its reverse side were called 'hutchies' or 'hoochies'. These provided the Durhams' living quarters. Second Lieutenant Sawbridge described them:

Hutchies were 6 feet by 6 feet by 12 feet deep. The Geordies, marvellous diggers, would simply dig a hole 6 feet by 6 feet until it reached the required depth. Then a prefabricated timber frame of 4 x 4 inch timber was lowered in the roof. Timbers were laid in position, and the earth returned to give 6 feet of overhead cover. Then from outside a trench was dug to find the hole. Once back inside, the walls were revetted with sandbags, empty beer boxes were let in to create a storage space, iron pickets were hammered into the walls to create bed frames. Some had wooden floors and my double hutchie was both my quarters and the platoon HQ with radio and telephone to Company HQ

For heating we used ammunition boxes with a sprinkling of sand in the bottom, on to which a drip-feed provided oil from a can of diesel oil on the roof some 5 to 6 feet above. They usually worked amazingly well and used very little oil to provide first-rate heat…there were holes in the sides of the ammunition boxes to allow the heat into the hutchies. To save space, beds were above one another – bunk beds. Steel girders formed the sides and the ends, with wire stretched diagonally across acting as the springs. On top we laid sleeping bags and we usually had 2 or 3 blankets apiece. There were normally 3 or 4 steps leading down into each hutchie from the adjoining trench.

The heating system, though relatively efficient, would not have passed a safety inspector back home, but it was essential for the Korean winter. However, it did claim one victim when Colour Sergeant Joseph Camby died of severe burns caused by an exploding heater on 5th January 1953.

Food was good. Self-heating cans of soup were favourites. A ring on the top of the can was part of a self-lighting fuse. When the ring was pulled, the fuse burnt away

Trench beautification, 1 DLI.

and boiled the soup in the can. Much of the food was American, with a great deal of turkey and fresh food, much of it very rich. C4 packs, usually supplied to the British, lasted one man for 24 hours or 4 men for one meal. Included in these were beans, tinned fruit, corned beef, cigarettes and sweets. The mixture of American food and the basic British Army rations was most successful and a bartering system was set up whereby the Americans exchanged their steaks, turkeys and chickens for much sought after puddings in the C4 packs, when festive and celebration periods occurred. Each platoon had its own cookhouse in a dugout.

Clothing - the basic uniform being green combat jacket and trousers - was also good, especially that issued for the severe Korean winter. This kept out the cold and was much envied by other UN units. Lance Corporal Alan Mavin:

You had a string vest, then an ordinary Army shirt & three pairs of Long Johns. The first pair, you had a slit up the front and the back, so you didn't have to take them off for following the calls of nature. The second pair were of a woolly material, which were worn over the top of the first pair. Then you wore your trousers. You had a cap

In a hutchie, Private McGee, 1 DLI.

comforter over your head, like a little muffler, which you turned inside out, like the Commandos did during WW2. Big boots - exceptionally large. You had a thick inner-sole and thick stockings to keep your feet warm. You had a Parka, which came over your body to keep you warm. Two pairs of gloves: one pair of woollen gloves, the other were like gauntlets but only had a finger and a thumb like mittens. You hardly got them through the trigger guard of the rifle.

Rats, however, were a problem. Second Lieutenant John Lightley:

After the cold the most hated feature of our life was the rats, which infested the trenches. They were everywhere - in walls and roofs, communication trenches and undergrowth. One Sergeant refused to sleep in his own 'hoochie' alone in case they jumped on his face. They were found in sleeping bags and regularly ran across the table when you were eating. Most 'hoochies' had leaking sandbag walls where attempts had been made to bayonet them. They were a serious health risk.

John Lightley also described the daily routine:

Our daily routine was based around 'stand to' at first light. This would normally be the only time the whole platoon was up and about together and we took the opportunity to hold "O" [Orders] Groups and deal with the essential administration. There were always stores to be collected: food, wire, steel pickets, sandbags and laundry and rubbish to be sent back. Passwords and air identification panels changed daily and sitreps [situation reports] were sent and received. There were always the inevitable problems of toothache, flu and so on, plus requests for men to go back to the mobile bath unit, or help with some task at Company Headquarters. We were never at full strength

During the day, Sergeant Charles McCoombe was in charge and a small number of men manned the Observation Post and did the administration. The rest of us went to sleep. At night, roles were reversed, when most people were up and working at various jobs, such as standing patrols, digging and wiring or sentry duties. In winter, because of the intense cold sentries and patrols had to be changed over at relatively short intervals. The Platoon Sergeant was usually awake and in charge during the day, whilst the Platoon Commander slept. The latter was in command during the night.

As in WW1, night was the time of greatest activity. Constant attention was given to the wire protecting the front of the company positions. Empty shell cases sealed & weighted at one end were used to hammer the pickets into the ground. To muffle the sound, the end was wrapped with sandbags, yet in the stillness of the night each thump seemed too loud for comfort. Regular checks of the wire were carried out,

Korean Porters.

particularly around the minefields, as there was always the risk that a patrol might stumble into a minefield in the dark, if the wire was broken. Fortifications were also constantly improved and overhead protection strengthened, with trenches deepened and repaired as necessary.

Korean porters, known to the Durhams as 'Noggies' or 'Gooks', carried the heaviest loads. Most could not speak English but quickly learned much used Army words like "f.....g" which, as they found difficulty pronouncing "f", came out as "ucking". In their turn, the soldiers picked up the odd Korean word and, between the two groups, were able to make some conversation, along with much banter. John Lightley again: *Each Company had a number of Korean porters who endeared themselves to the company by the great weight of supplies they could carry on the 'A' frames on their backs and by their loyalty and good humour. They could carry considerable loads - boxes of ammunition, jerry cans of water and diesel for the heaters.*

ON PATROL

Whenever the British soldier is in the front line, he seeks to dominate No Man's Land by active patrolling. The need to do this was just as important in Korea as it had been in past wars. Lieutenant Colonel Jeffreys wrote:

Patrolling...was the essence of the successful conduct of the defence. The enemy and our own positions were generally separated by a distance of 600 to 1000 yards, a paddy valley nearly always lay between the two positions; in a few notable cases trenches were only 100 to 300 yards apart and no valley intervening; these were obviously trouble spots. Our positions were on the whole well wired and surrounded by minefields. A night attack was therefore the best way to capture or raid these strong positions and the Chinese practically always used this method of attack. The aim of all patrolling was therefore as follows: To find out about the enemy's positions; to prevent the enemy finding out about our positions; to prevent the enemy attacking our positions without first having to run the gauntlet of our patrols; to get warning

Preparing for patrol. [from left] Private Walton, Private Reay & Lance Corporal Morgan, 1 DLI.

of an enemy attack.

Standing patrols were sent out by the front line company. The other patrols tended to be supplied by the reserve companies. Second Lieutenant Michael McBain wrote:

As a forward platoon, with no other friendly troops between us and the enemy, we would be expected to form one or sometimes two standing patrols in front of the position. These patrols would consist of a lance corporal or corporal and three privates. The patrol would leave the position just as it was getting dark, move through one of the wire corridors to a pre-selected location and remain there all night in the summer but probably for no more than two or three hours in the winter. The patrol had a radio or a field telephone and their task was to give early warning of an enemy attack, to report any other enemy movement and to act as an entry or exit point for other friendly patrols going out into No Man's Land.

Lieutenant Colonel Jeffreys described the importance of these patrols:

No standing patrol would come in in the face of enemy pressure without my express permission as Battalion Commander; if driven in it must be re-established as soon as possible. The withdrawal or loss of a standing patrol was the sign that would alert the whole Battalion. They were always dug in with several alternative positions - normally between 100 to 200 yards in front or flank of the major position. Passwords were regularly changed and very simple eg. 'Kellogs/Cornflakes' or 'Fish/Chips'. Patrols returning from No Man's Land had to know the current password to get past the standing patrol. The aid to navigation at night in No Man's Land was provided by the searchlight at Panmunjon, which shone vertically into the air over the site of the peace talks.

Fighting patrols wore armoured vests and went into No Man's Land to dominate the area by operating as ambush parties. Lieutenant Colonel Jeffreys:

Their strength was normally one Officer or Sergeant and 15 Other Ranks. Sometimes they were directed to sites overlooking or blocking routes which the enemy was likely to use; sometimes to tactical features which the enemy would probably visit. Always this site was chosen for its tactical suitability for the setting of an ambush. If, as darkness fell, the enemy beat you to an ambush site it meant that the enemy ambushed the ambush. And, so all through our periods in the line, there went on the grim game of "catching" the other chap while he was on the move and you were ready like an open trap.

Lieutenant David Dunn described the preparations for his first patrol:

My first major patrol was to the valley floor, leaving through 'B' Company lines. During the day Peter Hayes, the Intelligence Officer, with a Royal Artillery Forward

Observation Officer and I got into an Observation Post and Peter explained my route and mission. We selected defensive fire tasks in case I needed to be extricated and report lines and stage bounds were selected, timings were agreed, and I was wishing that I had paid more attention at Warminster. What had stuck in my mind was the acronym DEWARS [Dress, Equipment, Weapons, Ammunition, Rations and Security] as the basis for patrol orders.

It tipped down with rain that night and I reported to Reggie Atkinson, 'B' Company Commander. He was not best pleased at the dripping rain from my hat on to his map but we agreed to call the three streams in the paddy on my route as 'Tyne', 'Tees' and 'Wear'. Not original but easy to remember. The streams were in long neglected paddy and were of unknown depth. As patrol leader I was lowered into the water with my Sterling machine gun across my chest and the man behind me holding on to the sling until the bottom was reached. I was up to my nipples in unpleasant, smelly, slow moving water and feeling vulnerable when I was summoned to the radio by a 'Fetch Sunray' call from Reggie. "Have you reached 'Tyne' yet?" he said. "I'm in it up to my neck" I replied and I swear that I heard his dry chuckle.

A reconnaissance patrol consisted of two men whose task was to observe the enemy and report back. They would move out into No Man's Land just before first light, find a position from which enemy movement could be observed and return at dusk. It was normal for all patrols to come in via a different route to that used on the way out into No Man's Land. This was to ensure that no Chinese patrol, which may have spotted the outward route and placed an ambush on it, would succeed in its intentions.

Accidents occurred and several men were wounded or killed by what were described in the official documents as 'battle accidents.' In winter particularly, patrols had to exercise great care. Second Lieutenant Lightley:

A constant debate took place as to whether safety catches should be on or off. The problem is that in snow or ice, it was easy to slip or fall and the chance of accidentally firing off a burst from your Sten or Bren was quite high. I think we eventually compromised with about half the safety catches off when moving. Accidents like this or in minefields were very distressing but had to be an accepted risk under such conditions. Our first casualty was caused by someone throwing a grenade at a suspected enemy and catching the back of the trench with his hand so that it dropped at his feet. Fortunately, he and his companion were fairly agile and only one was wounded. After that we always threw a stone, in the belief that if it was an enemy patrol, they would react. If nothing happened it was probably the wind or an animal.

On patrol, Private Walcroft & Private Strugnell, 'D' Company , 1 DLI

Captain Clarke, MC had joined the battalion from the King's Shropshire Light Infantry. He was second-in-command of 'D' Company when it took up position on Point 159: *On arrival in Korea, 'D' Company was positioned on one of the forward hills facing the Chinese across the valley. Warfare then consisted of both sides patrolling No Man's Land in the valley with occasional raids by one side or the other on to positions opposite. Everyone was well dug in and although we relied on mines and barbed wire to keep the enemy out, they seemed to rely on being so well tunnelled into their hills, that even if you overran their position you would be lucky to find them as was proved by one of our raiding parties later. Before a raid on our position, their tactics were to shell the position very heavily to blast a way through the wire and minefields and follow up closely behind in waves, regardless of casualties, so we knew what to expect!*

'D' Company experienced its baptism of fire within a few days of arriving on the position. On 1ˢᵗ October, Lance Corporal Edward O'Brien was killed and Major Kelly and Privates J. Coley and E Timms were wounded. Lieutenant Dunn wrote after he joined the battalion in 1953 that: *Shelling by the Chinese became a way of life, even a spectator sport. Everyday at noon, the crew of a Centurion tank on a nearby hillside would leave their tank, batten down the hatches and disappear into their 'hutchies'. Not long after, four shells would fall on the tank position. The enemy went round the known tank positions with four shells, each in strict rotation. No wonder the activity was called 'the milk round.'*

Korea was not good tank ground with its steep hills and wet valleys, so it was usual to place a tank on top of a hill in each battalion position to give fire support when required.

Most of the time on Point 159 was spent repairing and strengthening the positions and in intensive patrolling. On the night of 4th/5th October, 1 DLI was relieved by the 1st Battalion Black Watch and moved to Area 7, north of the River Teal, and then on to Reserve Area 3. As well as training on night patrols and setting up ambushes, there was time for recreation and sport, particularly football, plus a show by Ted Ray and his party as part of the Commonwealth Services Entertainment. There was also work on a section of the Kansas Line, a reserve line that stretched across the width of Korea.

OPERATION BLAYDON

During the night of 31ˢᵗ October, the battalion relieved the Black Watch and returned to Point 159 and intensive patrolling began. On 1ˢᵗ November, an enemy mortar bomb wounded Private D. Torr and on 3ʳᵈ November, a 'C' Company patrol was fired on.

Second Lieutenant Sawbridge wrote:

The Chinese had a small fixed-wing aircraft, which used to fly over No Man's Land issuing messages through a loudspeaker - "Hello Black Watch," "How are you getting on King's?" "Enjoy your time out Fusiliers," "Welcome back Durhams," and

so on. They obviously had spies/infiltrators in the Commonwealth Division who were able to report back by radio. We never tried to shoot down the aircraft. We wanted to hear what 'little Jane' – as the voice was called – had to say and front line small arms would immediately bring down stonks from the Chinese. Planning then began for a major raid, codenamed 'Operation Blaydon'. Its objective was to enter the Chinese positions on Point 133, destroy their tunnels, kill the enemy and bring back a prisoner. Part of the plan was to place a lying-up patrol in a position close enough to the Chinese lines to ascertain their movements and identify objectives. This patrol took

Second Lieutenant Sawbridge, 1 DLI.

place on 6th November and was entrusted to Captain Clarke MC, who had earned the sobriquet 'Jungle Jim':

I was told to go and lie up behind the enemy positions on the hills opposite to observe their positions from the rear. I wasn't sure at first whether they were just trying to get rid of me or what! However, I was assured that I wouldn't have been asked to do this unless there was a very good reason for it. I was told I could choose anyone I liked from the company to go with me with the radio. I chose Private Smith, our company clerk.

As we were to lie on a feature on the other side of the valley, which appeared to be unoccupied and had very little cover on it, I made as sure as possible that Private Smith and I would be difficult to spot on this feature, which we were to reach by night, lie up by day observing the enemy and return the next night. So we tested ourselves out on the company against a hill background until I was satisfied we couldn't be seen. The code word for arriving in the position was something like 'Eagles Nest' and I was assured I wouldn't be worried by our own artillery.

After nightfall, we moved through the minefield gap and down to the valley floor, Private Smith dogging my footsteps, and then up the other side on to the 'baldy' hill and, as it began to get light, I made for a clump of bushes into which we settled with a view of the rear of the enemy position on the hill to our flank. All we could see was a black hole in the rear of the hill, which was the tunnel entrance to their positions on the hill above and, occasionally, we saw figures going in and out of it. The only danger was from our own shelling when bits of shrapnel flew across and landed near us on our hill! Needless to say we got back safely the next night.

Captain Clarke brought back a detailed sketch map of the objective - vital information for the forthcoming operation. This had been an extremely dangerous mission for one false move during the long hours of observation would have been disastrous.

Snow fell on the morning of 7th November followed by a dozen enemy shells at lunchtime due, according to Second Lieutenant Sawbridge, to *"7 Platoon frying chops with too much smoke"*. Lance Corporal A. Hedley was wounded. The following day, Privates R. Owen and R. Vinton were wounded by shelling and on 9th November, the Chinese shelled the road behind Point 159 and Second Lieutenant D. Constantine and Private G. Sandbrook were wounded.

Work continued on wiring and improving the defences, whilst on 18th November, the Chinese scattered propaganda leaflets and unfurled a banner saying "Don't die for the Yanks", which was later brought in by a 'B' Company patrol.

On the night of 20th November, Captain Eric Burini was ordered to take out a

Looking towards Point 133, Operation Blaydon's objective, November 1952.

reconnaissance patrol and find a start line for the forthcoming Operation Blaydon:

I went on a recce patrol with Corporal Moody, protected by a firm base of some 15 blokes. We were to recce what was deemed to be an inter-unit boundary along a narrow ridge and also to try and establish a safe start line for the raiding party. Once in the valley, every feature looked different and confusing but we did manage to establish which was the ridge we were to patrol. We left the firm base some 200yds from the foot of the ridge and began our recce; we firmly established that the ridge was unoccupied right back to its junction with the main range of hills. This took a long time because we had to move cautiously, try to keep below the skyline from either side and pause to listen occasionally. We did manage to establish a reasonably safe and adequate start line for the fighting patrol. We then left to rejoin our firm base and managed to get back to our line just as daylight broke.

On the night of 21ˢᵗ /22ⁿᵈ November, Second Lieutenant Barry Perrot and the raiding party from 'A' Company, followed Captain Burini and Corporal Moody, who had both been ordered not to join the raid, to the start line. There was some delay in getting the party organised on the start line. Captain Burini:

So I called on my radio, "Delay Blaydon, 5 minutes". Using a wireless in No Man's Land was fraught with problems, not least of which was the voice carry when speaking into the mike, so one tended to speak as quietly as possible and hope that acknowledgement was equally quiet. This, together with my unfortunate use of the word 'delay', caused a misunderstanding [sounded like 'relay'] and a few rounds of tank fire ploughed into the objective. A few moments later the attack got underway. The raid had been carefully planned and rehearsed. Lance Corporal Ernest Stockton: No.1 Platoon was taken to a hill that looked like Point 133. It was laid out with white tape to show us where the trenches were. We started to practice in daylight. Some men were stretcher-bearers and were made to carry someone back. It was hard going and we were kept at it. We were all knackered the first day. Then we had to do it at night. It was harder still but we had some good laughs, tipping each other off the stretchers. But the Don [Major Donoghue[] kept us at it. There were 32 of us with Sergeant Paddy Manning and our Platoon Commander, Second Lieutenant Perrot.

'A' Company Headquarters and No.3 Platoon, under the command of Major Donoghue MC, occupied a firm base to the south west of Point 133. No.1 Platoon under Second Lieutenant Perrot, who was later Mentioned in Despatches for his leadership, moved on to the start line. Any sound of movement was muffled by continuous machine gun fire. Once in position and ready to assault, Second Lieutenant Perrot was to send a codeword by wireless, which would bring down artillery and mortar fire on the objective. Later the raiding party would withdraw through the firm base on the completion of its task. Unfortunately, the few rounds previously fired by the tank probably warned the

Corporal Stockton, 'A' Company, 1 DLI.

33

Chinese of the impending raid.

As the party moved up the hill, the Chinese opened up with grenades and light machine gun fire and a number of casualties were suffered. On reaching the objective, it was found that the hill was encircled by a deep communication trench. This was so difficult to enter that it caused the raiders to break up into smaller parties that moved right and left down the trench. Only a brief glimpse was seen of Chinese disappearing through trapdoors and into their underground bunkers. It would have been extremely difficult and costly to attempt to follow them and would not have been possible by such a small raiding party. After a short time on the hill, the raiders, under heavy Chinese mortar and artillery fire, moved back through the firm base. Meanwhile, friendly artillery fire gave supporting cover to the withdrawing raiders.

Lance Corporal Ernest Stockton was involved in the raid:

Just as we were getting near their trenches, the Gooks [slang for Chinese soldiers] started firing LMG, Burp guns and grenades. The first two sections were hit bad and pinned down. Then Nick Carter stood up and shouted, "Come on lads, get up. Come on the Durhams." Some of the lads who had been wounded got up, but were wounded again - Smudger Smith was one of them. My section came through and into the trench. Just as I got in, I felt something go through the back of my beret. I thought I had been hit in the head. Then I saw Bill Kane just behind me. I said, "Bill, it's me Stocky." "It's not me," he shouted, "It's him." There was this Gook in the corner of the trench. We both shot at him and then remembered that we had to try and get a prisoner. Just then I fell over a body in the bottom of the trench. It was Wilkinson, one of my section, he had been hit in the head but he was starting to get up and was trying to go on. Just then we were given the order to withdraw. As I was getting out of the trench, a Gook, I don't know where he came from, ran right into me and onto my bayonet, knocking me back into the trench. I must have pulled the trigger of my Sten as we fell back and I got covered in blood. Just then Corporal Ronnie Harrison came along the trench wounded in both arms. We saw two Gooks go down a trap door. We had been told not to go into any trap doors, so I dropped two hand grenades in. Then they put the bloody searchlight on and the tanks started shooting again. You couldn't see a thing with that searchlight shining in your eyes. We walked, fell, rolled down that hill helping each other. Major Donoghue saw us and said, "Keep going, well done." Ronnie had been saved by his bullet proof vest. We all had one on that night, that's how he had only been hit in the arms. After that, we started back over the valley to 'C' Company lines and caught up with some of our lads with the stretchers and the badly wounded on them. I took some Stens from the walking wounded and then took over one end of a stretcher. When we got back to our side of the valley, there was a Sergeant waiting at the minefield gap. He just told us to keep going. He couldn't help us as he had to stay there to see the rest of the lads through. I went back to our position and got someone to help me with my clobber as it was frozen. I remember, I pissed in a tin and tipped it over the zip of my bullet proof vest so that I could undo it. It was what you call cold that night. We had hot food and drinks, changed our clothes and into bed. My 21ˢᵗ birthday was on the 24ᵗʰ November.

Lance Corporal Murray was a member of the Assault Pioneer Platoon, who accompanied the raiding party:

Our section commander came and said he had been given the task of blowing up an enemy position and he needed two volunteers to assist. Ralph Grimwood and myself stepped forward. I think Ralph would be twenty-two years old and a National Serviceman, and I was nineteen years old and a three-year Regular. One instruction was that any dead or wounded would be left until the task was completed then we would pick them up on the way back. We practiced this recovery in daylight until it was perfect. As the heavily armed force of youths filed through the minefield gap, the Colour Sergeant handed a pot of rum to each in turn. I drank as much as I could and it certainly warmed my guts.

We were climbing hard now; the Commonwealth tanks and guns were firing to give us cover. The attacking force started off in a sort of arrow head formation with us pioneers in the centre. I think with it being dark and us carrying a heavy load of explosives we climbed harder and ended up at the point of the patrol. A searchlight switched on from our side and looking up we saw a Chinese soldier coming from his shelter at the same time throwing a stick grenade at us. The Corporal killed him with his Sten gun, Ralph and I ducked with our dangerous load. The grenade went over my head and exploded close to Ralph and wounded him mainly, as I thought, round the eye but he could not walk.

A full scale battle was going on now with the Chinese on the run. The Corporal expected me to leave Ralph and pick him up on the way back. The searchlight had now gone out and it was dark, Ralph kept repeating, "Don't leave me Jim." I reassured him and bound up his eye at the same time screaming for the stretcher-bearers, who arrived very quickly and got him away. I then realised that the Corporal had gone. The first man I came to was still fighting, Lance Corporal Crinion. We located the objective, laid the charge and initiated the timing device. We heard a whistle being blown to indicate that we had taken prisoners and we withdrew off the hill.

At the debriefing, we were informed that the objective had been achieved, although the prisoners captured by the snatch parties were both dead, not having done that sort of thing before they did not know quite how hard to hit them on the head and they had overdone it. The Corporal was verbally reprimanded for leaving his men but, as he had only twenty odd days to do, no other action was taken. I was also reprimanded for sending Ralph back against orders. My reply was as it was a dark night, how were we to find our wounded especially if they had gone into coma, and who would vouch that we would return over the same stretch of ground that we came in on.

Private Bryan Dolman was one of those wounded during the raid:

When I was wounded, blackness came over me. It was a strange feeling of calmness, which started in my legs, then came upwards. When I came to, there were explosions going on all around. Then Corporal Ronnie Moore appeared. He asked me if I could stand. I managed to stand on my right leg with great difficulty. He carried me a short way, when he fell. I went rolling down the hill for a short distance, then he dragged me down to the bottom of the hill. He was saying all the time that I had to get back to Ann, my girlfriend. When we reached the valley, he lifted me onto his back and carried me. We fell many times in the paddy fields. I lost consciousness a number of times. When we reached the small river in the valley, I stuck my head into the water and drank as much as I could. By then it was breaking daylight. We struggled on till we reached the bottom of our position, then Ronnie left me and went for assistance. A party came and dressed my left leg and right foot. An officer pushed a pocket warmer into my hands as I was freezing. I was then put on front of a jeep and taken to the 60th Indian Field Ambulance, then by helicopter to the US 8055 MASH Hospital. Then flown to the British Commonwealth Hospital at Kure, Japan.

Corporal Ronald Moore was awarded the Military Medal. His citation included:

When the order to withdraw was signalled by his platoon commander, [he] went down the hill and set about organising the evacuation of his men... On finding that one man, Private Dolman, who he knew had been severely wounded in both legs by a grenade, was missing he went back to search for him, although the patrol at this time was still being engaged with small arms fire and grenades and the situation was very confused. When he found him close to the enemy position...he began to drag the wounded man down the hill, stopping more than once on the way... At this time our own artillery defensive fire also started to fall around him. Undeterred, Corporal Moore succeeded in dragging the wounded man clear of our own and the enemy's fire. On reaching the bottom of the hill, Corporal Moore discovered that his platoon had withdrawn. He therefore lifted Private Dolman on his back and carried him the 800 yards across the valley, arriving at the forward positions of his battalion over an hour after the remainder of the party. He successfully accomplished this in spite of the weight of the wounded man, who was much bigger than himself and in the face of enemy artillery and defensive fire.

'A' Company casualties were 13 wounded. These, in addition to Privates Dolman and Grimwood, included Privates A. Ball [also Mentioned in Despatches], T. Chalder, C. Garbutt, W. Grose, J. Hannah, R. Hodge, J. Holcombe, L. Webb, R. Wilkinson, N. Smith [K.O.Y.L.I.], Corporal R. Harrison and Lance Corporal. F. Wood.

Three men were also missing and presumed killed in action. These were, Private Dennis Baker, Private Douglas Bence and Lance Corporal Ronald Carwood. The next day patrols went out to search for the bodies. Private Baker was found but the other two men remained missing and their bodies were never found despite a diligent search.

Christmas Dinner, 1952.

As the raid had failed to take a prisoner, 'Operation Willington' was organised to take place on the night of 30th November with the objective of succeeding where 'Blaydon' had failed. The raiding party was provided by 'D' Company under the command of Second Lieutenant MacGregor-Oakford. No prisoner was taken, the Chinese again disappearing into their tunnels, and the raiders were subjected to heavy enemy shelling

On 1st December, 1 DLI was relieved by the 1st Battalion Duke of Wellington's Regiment. It snowed as the Durhams moved back to No. 3 Area and began working on the 'Kansas Line'. Digging in the winter conditions was far from easy. Sergeant Alf Mason, Signal Platoon:

Winter has set in with a vengeance. The ground is 4ft. deep in frost and a new latrine is required. Pick-axe points turn upwards. So Sergeant Wimpy Coxon brings his Assault Pioneer Platoon to bear – with explosives. Wally Spires is standing at the entrance to the Sergeants' Mess, watching the activities, from about 200 yards distance, when one explosion caused an egg-sized boulder to fly and hit Wally on the kneecap. He was eventually discharged 'unfit.'

The Durhams celebrated Christmas 1952 in No. 3 Area. The usual dinner was served with the bonus of free beer provided by the Australians and the 'Daily Mail'.

From Point 210 to Camp Casey

During the night of 27th/28th December, the Durhams relieved the 1st Battalion Royal Fusiliers on Point 210. It was bitterly cold. This position had received a great deal of damage from Chinese artillery and mortar fire and the first task was to improve it. Extensive digging and rewiring took place and the Command Post and platoon cookhouses were re-sited. On 30th December, Private David Davies was killed in a battle accident and Privates W. Holden and J. Power were wounded the next day by mortar fire. More snow fell on New Year's Day.

The minefields always gave great concern, particularly as the mines moved. Many lay on the slopes immediately in front of the trenches. In wet weather, some tended to slip and alter position. Also enemy artillery and mortar fire destroyed the markers

Major Donoghue MC with some soldiers from 'A' Company, 1 DLI.

and patrols moving in and out of the line had to proceed with great caution. Inevitably, there were accidents. On 2nd January 1953, Major Pat Donoghue MC was killed and three soldiers were wounded when they stumbled into the minefield. Aged 38, Major Donoghue had won his MC in World War 2. He was greatly respected as a firm but fair officer and a fine leader. As Private Ernie Dobson recalled *"If he couldn't do it, you couldn't do it"*. Major Jim Loveridge took over the command of 'A' Company on the death of Major Donoghue. Major Taylor replaced him in command of 'S' Company.

Digging in the rock hard ground and in plummeting temperatures was extremely difficult. Captain Burini:

It was getting very cold. The only way to dig was to put some petrol on the ground, light it, and when it had stopped burning, dig the bit that had softened and start again.

On 16th January, the body of a Royal Fusilier was brought in from No Man's Land. Captain Burini:

We took over from the Royal Fusiliers. These had been in a rather severe battle and

Camp Casey, Korea.

they had had quite a number of casualties. We brought one in. Six lads were used to pick this chap up. He was bloated because he had been out for some time and he was frozen stiff. We got him in eventually but it was a bit dicey. Later, it was discovered that one or two bodies had been booby-trapped.

Active patrolling and enemy fire accounted for a number of casualties over this period on Point 210. Private John Clements, with a patrol of 'D' Company, died of wounds on 7th January. On 20th January, Private Dennis Cresswell was killed in an accident picking up a Chinese grenade that exploded in his hands. On 24th January, another battle accident killed Private William Thomas, whilst Private Ronald Eacott was killed and three men were wounded on 27th January.

On the night of 29th/30th January, the Durhams were relieved by the 3rd Battalion 9th Infantry Regiment of the 2nd U.S. Division. This handover was described by Second Lieutenant Lightley:

Normally within the Commonwealth Brigade, these went smoothly, but, when we left, the Americans took over. The first problem was that they had more men than us and every slit trench and 'hoochie' was overflowing with men and extra equipment. The next was that 4 Platoon was to move out in an open truck. It was snowing and very cold, so that we had to stop every few minutes and march for a while to keep warm. The last straw was when the Americans began to fire flares and all their weapons, so that we believed that they had been attacked. The prospect of going back to help them out was not at all popular. Fortunately, it was all a false alarm but, no doubt, the Chinese found it interesting.

Lieutenant Sawbridge later recalled that 56 Americans took over a position held by 36 Durhams, though they were impressed

Durhams & Australians watching a show.

with the cleanliness and strength of the trenches.

1 DLI now found itself in a major rest camp, named Camp Casey. First impressions were far from good. It was a large camp capable of accommodating a division at rest. Tents, each holding 14 men, were provided with the only huts used as dining halls, cookhouses and a cinema. In the wet and bitterly cold weather, the camp was a sea of mud and extremely dirty and bleak. Lieutenant Colonel Jeffrey's immediate orders were to clean up the whole battalion area. There was much to be done. The latrines overflowed and stank and the ground was fouled, so new trenches were dug. Canteens and messes were organised and tent inspections took place. Training involved drills, exercises and weapons firing, plus there were necessary guard duties. Keeping fit was important and sports such as hockey and soccer were organised. There were also leisure activities, including films and a show with the singer Lizabeth Webb and a UK Concert Party.

During service in Korea, some leave was given to all ranks. This was officially known as 'R & R' - Rest and Recuperation - but quickly became known as 'I & I' - Intercourse and Intoxication. Captain Burini:

We were lucky enough to be sent to Tokyo for the five day break. The whole city seemed to be geared to pander to the sex instinct - the beer was good too! Turkish baths were the most sought after and of prime importance for the removal of the Korean grime, with the added attraction of scantly clad masseuses.

At the end of March 1953, a draft of 94 Korean soldiers joined the battalion. Their tasks were the same as the rest of the Durhams and they wore British uniform with green berets and the DLI cap badge.

Korean soldiers wearing the DLI cap badge, 1953.

On Point 355 - Little Gibraltar

On 6th April, the Commonwealth Division relieved the 2nd American Division on Point 355 – also known as 'Little Gibraltar.'

Lance Corporal Alan Mavin remembered the handover:

The Corporal said, "You two in there." We got in and it was jamb-packed with Americans. So we got in and were talking to them. After a while one of the Americans said, "Where's the rest of the fellows?" I said, "We're here, me and him." It was dead of night, quiet. A loud speaker from the enemy lines came on - "Welcome, officers and men of The Durham Light Infantry, we're going to play a record for you." They knew before we went in.

'Little Gibraltar' was a very steep and rocky hill about 1000 feet high, dominating the surrounding positions and a crossing of the Imjin River. It had to be held. Supplying the battalion on this hill was not easy and all food, ammunition and equipment had either to be carried up the steep slopes by Korean porters or by a winch railway known as the 'Flying Fox'. The trenches on 'Little Gibraltar' were hewn out of the solid rock and when it rained these became channels of mud and water. Later the sun dried the mud to dust, which then blew and covered everything. However, firm trench discipline ensured three meals a day, dry living

The summit of Little Gibraltar – Point 355, Korea.

quarters and a fair degree of comfort considering the front line position.

Once again it was essential to dominate No Man's Land. Active patrolling began immediately and there were a number of clashes until this domination was established. Captain Burini's first patrol was not without incident:

When we first took over Point 355, the Americans were being ambushed in their own minefield gaps. So the first thing we had to do was to put this right. It was customary for American patrols to take a mobile telephone with them as a secondary means of communication. This required hundreds of yards of combat cable, which was run out behind the patrol and, as a result, thickly carpeted the minefield gaps. On my first night out with a fighting patrol, I was followed very closely by my batman, Tommy [Tubby] Hall, a five foot tall miner from Seaham. He was festooned with flak jacket, six Sterling magazines and two pouches of the portable wireless as well as his own weapon.

As we were gingerly creeping through the minefield gap, he caught his foot in the cable and took off, landing with an almighty crash. A deathly and extremely nervous hush followed. After a few seconds, Tommy Hall gave his opinion of the Americans and their cable, very colourfully and in a loud voice enough to awaken any nearby Chinaman. He was eventually persuaded to calm down and we continued on our way. While still in the gap we were suddenly confronted with a hanging sign across our path warning us that mines were present. This caused a great deal of consternation, which was eventually resolved by stepping over the sign and keeping fingers crossed.

The US Airforce bombed the Chinese positions opposite on Point 227 for two hours. It proved to be a spectacular sight but there was some concern that some bombs might fall on the Durhams. Fortunately, this did not happen.

Again there were casualties. Corporal Hwang Po Joon of KATCOM [one of the Korean soldiers attached to the battalion] was killed on 11th April. On 16th April, Lieutenant Edmond Radcliffe failed to return from patrol and a search party failed to find his body. Private Joseph Naisbitt was killed on 27th April. Whilst on 2nd May, Lance Corporal Brian Bedford was killed in action and four other ranks were wounded.

Lance Corporal Robert Stockton was awarded the Military Medal. As second-in-command of a rifle section of 'A' Company, he had shown a consistently high standard of efficiency and gallantry over a period of six months. His citation included:

One particular instance occurred on the night of 4/5 May when Lance Corporal Stockton was a member of a reconnaissance/fighting patrol. When in the valley, the patrol was ambushed by a large party of the enemy, which well outnumbered them.

The enemy quickly took advantage of his strength and attempted to outflank our patrol. A fierce fire fight ensued. Before being completely surrounded the patrol commander ordered his men to withdraw. This they did, taking with them five of their own wounded. Lance Corporal Stockton, who was near one of his own platoon who had been wounded in the head and was unconscious, remained where he was and continued to fight. The enemy crawled to within a few yards of his position and he accounted for no fewer than five of them with his own Sten gun. During the skirmish, which followed the withdrawal of our own troops, Lance Corporal Stockton lay quiet and when the remaining enemy had retired he proceeded to carry his

Track up to Little Gibraltar, Korea.

unconscious companion back across open and difficult country, and along a minefield of which he had little knowledge, until he finally reached our own lines some two hours later.

Lance Corporal Stockton was actually from The King's Own Yorkshire Light Infantry but had volunteered to join the Durhams in Korea. There were several other officers and men from the other Light Infantry Regiments who served with 1 DLI in Korea. Among the casualties of 5th May was Private John Hall who was killed in a battle accident. The rest of May was taken up with patrols and shelling and mortaring. On 30th May, three men were wounded, Private James Eggett [KOYLI] died of wounds and Private Donald Hargreaves [KOYLI] was killed in action.

3rd June 1953 was Coronation Day. Captain Burini described how it was celebrated:

'A' Company was in reserve beneath the main peak. On the night before, a patrol led by Lieutenant Bill Knott-Bower had gone across the valley to the Chinese positions and laid out some yellow and red fluorescent aircraft recognition panels in the form of 'EIIR' about ten metres in front of the Chinese forward trenches. So the first thing we saw at daybreak were these panels that stood out brilliantly.

About half way through the morning, every 25- pounder gun in the Commonwealth Division began firing red, white and blue smoke on the Chinese lines in front of us. While this was going on, the men in the forward positions jumped on to the trench parapets and gave three cheers for Her Majesty. There was some concern that the Chinese might take advantage of the cover provided by the smoke and attack us, but they behaved themselves and probably thought that we were all mad.

A celebration parade was also held in a rear area of which 'A' Company provided a detachment under my command, the highlight of which was a march past the President of South Korea. After last light, a searchlight was shone on our Regimental Flag flying from the flagpole and a group of our buglers played the Regimental calls grouped around the flag in full view of the Chinese, who once again did nothing – much to the relief of the buglers!

A great deal of patrolling took place in the early days of June. It was essential to hold Little Gibraltar and early warning of enemy intentions was vital. Capt Burini described one of these patrols:

Patrolling was the main occupation when the battalion was in the line. Patrols were frequent and had to be carefully controlled to avoid friendly clashes on dark nights. Three fighting patrols went out under the command of a small command group. Corporal Moody and I were detailed as control of one of these groups on an evening of very heavy mist. We decided that the mist was useful cover to enable us to get out in daylight and find a really good lie up position. We were shortly joined by the three fighting patrols that were spaced out along two spurs on either side of us; and there we sat until it was nearly dawn. The main problem was keeping awake for that length of time. Sometime during our vigil, David Margett's patrol thought they saw movement in front and asked me to call for artillery fire. We had the New Zealand gunners in support and they were a very efficient and supportive bunch but, even so, I felt I had to be cautious about gunfire, so it took some time before the guns fired for effect. When they did the rounds exploded dreadfully close to us.

About an hour before dawn, we were ordered back to base, easier said than done, and the trickiest part of the operation. We were given heavy machine gun covering fire [more to cover our own noise than protective] and I got them all moving. Moody and I decided to wait for Margett's patrol to escort us back to base and had a dicey time trying to make sure that approaching figures were indeed our blokes without giving our own position away and avoiding being shot by mistake. We made it but a few nights later [10th June] on a similar operation, Johnny Tresawna was killed at precisely that difficult time by Chinamen who appeared in front of him after the fighting patrols had gone.

Enemy action against the battalion positions on 5th June, resulted in the death of Sergeant Ralph Liddle and the wounding of Private J. Barker. On 8th June, Private Samuel Cotton was killed in action and Private D. Jones was wounded on the following day. In addition to the death of Major John Tresawna, Corporal T. Allen and Private W. Toomey were wounded on the 10th June - Private Toomey for the second time.

Second Lieutenant John Grubb, a National Service officer aged 18 years who had only been with the battalion for four days, was seriously wounded on 16th June, when an enemy mortar bomb exploded on the trench parapet. He died of his wounds shortly afterwards. Second Lieutenant T. Gordon, who had come out to Korea with John Grubb, was wounded by the same bomb. Second Lieutenant David Peat, also newly arrived, was later quoted in the 'Evening Chronicle':

John Grub volunteered for the DLI because he knew it would lead to a Korea posting. He was very good company and we did a lot together. I particularly remember when he was in Durham that we visited a workingmen's club at Oakenshaw and we had a helluva night. The hospitality was excellent. I later returned there and had a quiet moment with the people he had met.

'D' Company was holding the line when the most serious attacks on the battalion by the enemy took place over three nights starting on 19th June. Then Lieutenant Colonel

DLI flag flying over Little Gibraltar, Korea.

Jeffreys' tactic of putting out strong and alert patrols paid great dividends in holding and then breaking up these attacks. On the night of 19th/20th June, an ambush patrol from No.10 Platoon under the command of Second Lieutenant Hill was attacked by 20 to 30 enemy in an area known as Alice Springs. After a brief fire fight the enemy withdrew having suffered several casualties. The following night was quiet.

On the night of 21st /22nd June, No.10 Platoon again provided an ambush patrol of 14 men in the same area. This patrol, led by Sergeant McCabe, was organised into a control group [Sergeant McCabe and his wireless operator, each carrying Sten guns and grenades] and two sections – each led by a NCO with five men, carrying three Bren guns, three Stens plus grenades. At 2215 hours, the patrol was attacked. An account latter appeared in the Regimental Journal:

After some five minutes the shapes of five enemy were seen creeping over the crest of the hill. This party was immediately engaged and three were seen to fall. At the same time a larger party was heard moving up the hill, through the minefield, to cut off the ambush from Surry Hills. A shower of stick grenades were thrown onto the hill, wounding two members of the ambush. Sergeant McCabe then regrouped and faced towards the large enemy group. This group was met by concentrated fire as it reached the crest. However, although severe casualties were inflicted on the enemy, their numbers were stronger than the ambush. Sergeant McCabe then started to withdraw to Surry Hills. During the withdrawal, Lance Corporal MacDonald remained as a rearguard with a Bren to cover the withdrawal.

Private Choung Si Ko, of KATCOM, was killed with Privates P. Bunn, T. Reed and G. Male and Corporal K. Dawes wounded. The enemy fired on the likely lines of withdrawal with mortar bombs but there were no further casualties.

No.11 Platoon provided the ambush patrol on Alice Springs on the night of 22nd/23rd

Warning sign on Little Gibraltar, Korea.

June, under the command of Second Lieutenant Cunningham. Four men under the command of Corporal Robert Lofthouse were placed on the shoulder of the hill to protect the main patrol from being surprised by the enemy. The night was dark and a constant drizzle made visibility poor. Again an account appeared later in the Regimental Journal:

At 2200 hours the party on top of Alice Springs observed two enemy moving forward towards the empty weapon pits. Having ascertained that the pits were empty and presuming the hill unoccupied, the enemy waved for the rest of the group to come up on to the hill, which they did, in all some 12 men. Corporal Lofthouse, showing great patience, waited for this party to bunch, which eventually they did. He then opened fire at short range and the stillness of the night was shattered by the chatter of the Brens and Stens and the ripping noise peculiar to the enemy burp gun. Every now and again the noise was punctuated by the sharper crack of exploding grenades. Half the enemy party was killed. The remainder fled down the hill. A larger group then assaulted the hill and, again, Corporal Lofthouse coolly engaged them and then withdrew off the hill to the main ambush position, closely followed by the enemy. Once Lofthouse's party had rejoined the ambush, Second Lieutenant Cunningham opened heavy small arms fire on the enemy who dispersed having suffered heavy casualties.

Corporal Robert Lofthouse was wounded in this action but stayed on to control the fire of his small group. He had served for eight months in Korea and had carried out 28 patrols. He was described in the citation for the award of the Military Medal as "a most skilful, resourceful and fearless leader."

As this action was being fought, another group of the enemy attacked the standing patrol on the 'Nose' feature. This patrol was forced to withdraw under the enemy pressure but successfully reached the main position bringing with them their two wounded.

The enemy was now pressing home his attacks on the ambush patrol with considerable courage. Another group, about 30 strong, appeared on the left flank of the patrol's position. A heavy fire fight began and, again, the enemy was driven off with heavy casualties. By now the ambush patrol had suffered 50% casualties with Second Lieutenant Cunningham amongst the wounded. As the officer prepared to withdraw his patrol, he found to his consternation that another superior enemy force was blocking the route from Alice Springs to Surry Hills. Second Lieutenant Cunningham regrouped his men and prepared to fight it out where he was.

This enemy force moved off to assault Surry Hills, having first detached a small force to attack the standing patrol on Cobar. This patrol under the command of Lance Corporal Rosevear fought off the enemy, who then retired leaving behind two bodies. The main enemy assault on Surry Hills failed after fierce fighting in which three defenders were badly wounded. At this point, Second Lieutenant Cunningham, seeing the enemy withdrawing from Surry Hills, moved his patrol into the Hills, carrying the wounded with them. The whole of 'D' Company's position was now heavily mortared by the enemy with some 1500 bombs, of which over 500 fell on Surry Hills. Over 20 Durhams were wounded on 23rd June. These men were moved quickly and efficiently through two medical posts, one at No.12 Platoon Command Post and the other in the cookhouse at No.11 Platoon. A wiring party from 'A' Company, working in No.12 Platoon area, became stretcher bearers ensuring that No.12 Platoon remained in position at full strength.

Private Ronald Cottingham was killed in this action. Amongst the wounded were Privates D. Cotton, R. Brown, J. Broadhurst, G. Maddison, G. Oughton, J. Pearson, C. Rawnsley, J. Spooner, L. Thompkins, H. Wood and Lance Corporal G. Macdonald. Private Ted Jones was also wounded:

That evening I was put into an ambush patrol, No.2 on the Bren Gun to George Broadbent and we went out of the line after dark. We were in No Man's Land for a few hours when all hell was let loose – firing, mortar bombs from all angles. – some of our own dropping short probably. I remember slinging six hand grenades, which were on my breast straps as I did not want them exploding on me. By now dawn was just beginning to break and I got hit on the right side of my neck and shoulder. My immediate thought was that this could not happen to me, I must get out of here. I tried to walk but my legs seemed to be going past my head. I realised later that I was on my back, unable to walk.

Eventually, I was picked up by the stretcher bearers. I remained conscious while they got me back in the trenches but I thought the right side of my face had gone and I appeared to be breathing through a hole in my neck. I was told I was picked up by helicopter and taken to the 43rd MASH behind the line. It was found that the shrapnel had penetrated my neck and had plunged down and punctured my lung, leaving a lot of fluid. After many more days, I was flown to Tokyo and then by ambulance to the British Commonwealth General Hospital. I was put into an Australian Ward and the nursing staff were superb and really cared for us.

Second Lieutenant J. Parker was commanding a fighting patrol from 'A' Company, which had been sent out at 0100 hours to sweep Alice Springs. His mission was successful but, on returning to base, an enemy mortar bomb landed in the midst of the patrol wounding him and six soldiers.

The importance of these actions was summed up by the writer in the Regimental Journal:

The company position provided the most obvious stepping stone for the capture of the whole of Point 355. It had been previously successfully attacked by the enemy when held by another unit. On that occasion the enemy had formed up close in front of the position and rushed it before our artillery, mortars and small arms could make their weight felt. Our plan was, therefore, to engage the enemy with mobile outposts or ambushes and standing patrols in front of the main position. This would enable us to prevent the enemy forming up close to the main position and give our mortars and artillery the chance to destroy him before he could close. This plan was undoubtedly most successful.

The enemy had received a bloody nose. His attempts to clear No Man's Land of the standing and ambush patrols and then launch a major attack on Little Gibraltar had failed in spite of superior numbers. His casualties had been very heavy and this was to be the last serious attack on the battalion's positions.

'D' Company, which had performed so splendidly, was relieved on the night of the 28th/29th June. Second Lieutenant Cunningham was awarded the Military Cross. Private Rawlings was awarded the Military Medal and Lance Corporal Rosevear was Mentioned in Despatches. Major Robert Scott, commanding 'D' Company, was awarded the Military Cross. His citation outlines the methods he used in fighting the enemy:

He and his company were seen to particular advantage when holding the left forward position on Pt. 355 in the summer of 1953. During this time the company was subjected to severe shelling and to a succession of probing actions by the enemy. Major Scott established a permanent ambush on a position two hundred and fifty yards in front of his main position. He also found another outpost of section strength a little further in. His three standing patrols completed the screen with which he fought the enemy with great skill and determination on three successive nights. The screen, handled with great boldness, foiled all efforts by the enemy to close on the main position itself. In turn it inflicted, in three nights of heavy fighting, at least sixty casualties by small arms fire and many more through the direction of its supporting artillery and, in spite of the fluid hand-to-hand nature of the fighting, not one wounded man or dead body was left to the enemy.

At the end of June, the Durhams moved to Yong Dong and by mid July were in divisional reserve. Further awards included the OBE to Major 'Reggie' Atkinson, commanding 'A' Company. According to the citation, he had displayed *"the highest standard of devotion to duty and efficiency"* throughout the campaign. It went on to say: *Although his company had at least as many if not more shells on it than any other company during its period in the lines, the casualties sustained by it in the trenches were far the lightest; this was due to its industrious and efficient digging and its high standard of battle discipline. Major Atkinson provided the inspiration and drive which ensured both factors...*

Second Lieutenant MacGregor-Oakford MC.

Second Lieutenant Robert MacGregor-Oakford was awarded a well-earned Military Cross. The citation included:

Since the Battalion first arrived in Korea, 2/Lieutenant MacGregor-Oakford has commanded the same platoon. During this time he has carried out more than thirty patrols and one raid. His platoon has frequently found itself in most unpleasant positions, notably on Pt. 159 and in the left forward Company on Pt. 355. In spite of having much more than his share of shelling and a steady drain on his strength through casualties, he has by his own vigorous leadership and cheerfulness always kept his platoon's morale and fighting efficiency high and his position in good order. Good though his work in the main position has been it is in the realm of patrolling that he has made an outstanding mark. All his many patrols have been marked by a combination of shrewd cunning, sound planning and great daring. The conduct in battle of this young National Service officer has throughout been on a very high level indeed and proved a stimulating example to his platoon and in fact his whole Company.

Mayor of Durham's Korea Fund parcels.

Captain J. Tonkinson, Signals Officer and, later, Adjutant, received the MBE for *his "great enthusiasm, energy and determination to overcome all difficulties...His drive and skill ensured a high standard of communications despite the most trying conditions."*
Casualties continued throughout July, largely caused by artillery and mortar fire. On 9th July, Privates R. Jeffrey and J. McKenzie were wounded. Captain P. de Greenwell, Sergeant A. Peacock and Private A. Booth were wounded on the following day. On the 11th, Lieutenant C. Bower was wounded and Private John Rowson was killed. Finally on 17th July, Private Barry Gardiner was killed and Private Peter Million mortally wounded – the last Durham fatalities in Korea.
On the 24th July, with peace less than a week away, the Chinese launched an attack on a feature known as Jane Russell, which was held by US Marines. The battalion then in reserve was ordered to be ready to help if need arose. Captain Burini:
The situation soon became fluid and uncertain, so we found ourselves called out to support the Americans. My platoon eventually found itself going through minefield

gaps. Going through the gap, I heard a voice to my right coming from the minefield and a couple of our lads crouching in the gap told me that Private Savage had wandered into the field and had stood on a mine. They did not know how badly hurt he was but had sent for assistance. My platoon was in position near by, so I stayed to help keep him company.

After 15 minutes or so, an Engineer Captain came along, asked where Private Savage was and immediately began probing his way into the minefield with a bayonet. We held one end of a roll of white tape, which he ran out as a guide for his return.

I later visited Savage in hospital in Kure, Japan, I found that he had his leg blown off, part of one hand was missing and one of his eyes was damaged.

Private Savage was the final battalion casualty in Korea and must have been one of the last casualties from the Commonwealth Division. The US Marines beat off the enemy attack without the need to call on the Durhams for assistance.

At 22.00 hours on 27th July 1953, the battalion's bugles sounded the ceasefire. For the Durhams, the Korean War was over. Lieutenant David Dunn remembered:

[from left] Privates Brown, Haig, Jennings & Newman after the truce, August 1953.

We counted the 48 hours down and were amazed that at 4.00 pm on the afternoon when a ceasefire was due to start at midnight, the US Air Force was still dropping napalm on Chinese positions and the Chinese were still shelling American and South Korean positions but the 'milk round' stopped and, by report, not a single shell landed in the Commonwealth Division area in the last 24 hours of the war.

Twenty-four officers and men were killed or died of wounds whilst serving with the 1st Battalion The Durham Light Infantry in the Korean War. Some of these were attached to the DLI from other regiments. In addition, three men were reported missing and presumed dead, as their bodies were never found in spite of searches. A final search was made for Lieutenant Ratcliffe who had gone missing on 16th April 1953. Lieutenant David Dunn:

My last day near the front was spent on the valley floor below Point 355 with a search party and a body bag looking for the last remains of Edmund Ratcliffe who had not returned from patrol and had not been among those who passed through the returned Prisoner of War Camp. Our search was in vain and it was a depressing note on which to leave the front knowing that a comrade was still there.

Records also show that a total of 124 officers and men were wounded.

In August, the battalion moved back from the Kansas Line and was ordered to dig a fall back position on the Jamestown Line. 'A' Company meanwhile moved to Britannia Camp, which had been set up as a reception area for returning POWs.

In September 1953, just before the battalion boarded the 'Empire Orwell' and left Korea for the last time, one important duty remained. At Pusan, the Durhams paraded for a memorial service in the UN Military Cemetery and, on that very emotional day, said goodbye to their comrades who had made the supreme sacrifice and who would not be returning home.

Grave of Major Donoghue MC, Pusan, 1953.

DEDICATION

This small book is dedicated to Brigadier Peter Jeffreys DSO, OBE and the officers and other ranks who served with the 1st Battalion The Durham Light Infantry in Korea from September 1952 to September 1953, and in remembrance of those who gave their lives in this war for democracy and freedom.

ROLL OF HONOUR

Lance Corporal Edward O'Brien	1st October 1952
Private Dennis Ernest Baker	22nd November 1952
Private David Davies	30th December 1952
Major Charles Patrick Donoghue MC	2nd January 1953
Colour Sergeant Joseph Graham Camby	5th January 1953
Private John Alan Clements	7th January 1953
Private Dennis Reginald Cresswell	20th January 1953
Private William Henry Thomas	24th January 1953
Private Ronald Eacott	27th January 1953
Corporal Hwang Po Joon [Korean]	11th April 1953
Private Joseph Naisbitt	27th April 1953
Lance Corporal Brian Bedford	2nd May 1953
Private John Wilfred Hall	5th May 1953
Private James Eggett	30th May 1953
Private Donald Hargreaves	30th May 1953
Sergeant Ralph Liddle	5th June 1953
Private Samuel George Cotton	8th June 1953
Major John Anthony Tresawna DSO	11th June 1953
Second Lieutenant John Raymond Grubb	16th June 1953
Private Choung Si Ko [Korean]	22nd June 1953
Private Ronald Cottingham	24th June 1953
Private John Rowson	11th July 1953
Private Barry Frank Gardiner	17th July 1953
Private Peter Million	17th July 1953

MISSING

Lance Corporal Ronald Douglas Carwood	22nd November 1952
Private Douglas Mervyn Bence	22nd November 1953
Lieutenant Edmond Lyons Willoughby Ratcliffe	16th April 1953

DECORATIONS

The following is a list of decorations and awards taken from records available. It includes awards to men who were seconded to the DLI. It is hoped that this list is complete

Bar to Distinguished Service Order [DSO]
Lieutenant Colonel P.J. Jeffreys DSO, OBE

Order of the British Empire [OBE]
Major R.G. Atkinson MC [& Bar]

Military Cross [MC]
2/Lieutenant J.C.H. Cunningham [KOYLI]
2/Lieutenant R.B. MacGregor-Oakford
Captain J.G. Pearce [KSLI]
Major R.E.G. Scott

Military Medal [MM]
Corporal R. Lofthouse [KOYLI]
Corporal R.A. Moore
Private D. Rawlings
L/Corporal R.J. Stockton [KOYLI]

Member of the British Empire [MBE]
W.O.2 G.A. Calvert
W.O. 2 C.H. Gibbens
Captain J.B. Tonkinson

British Empire Medal [BEM]
Sergeant J.R. Coxon

Mentioned In Despatches [MID]

Corporal T.G. Allen
Private A.H. Ball
W.O.2 L. Beirne
Captain E.B. Burini
W.O.2 F.A. Elliott [KSLI]
2/Lieutenant S.H. Hall [KOYLI]
Captain P.S. Hayes [Ox&Bucks]
Corporal J.G. Murray
Lieutenant W.J. Nott-Bower
2/Lieutenant B.D. Perrott
L/Corporal D.A.H. Rosevear
2/Lieutenant E.H.F. Sawbridge
Major R.E.G. Scott
Corporal R. Shannon
Corporal D. Stokes